A SPECIAL GIFT

PRESENTED TO

Kelly (MVP) Johnson

FROM

CLC

DATE

June 3rd '07

PRINCIPLES FOR A LIFETIME OF SUCCESS

GRADUATE *to* GREATNESS

A LIFE COMMENCEMENT MESSAGE

ANDREW JAMES
WITH AN INTRODUCTION BY
JOHN C. MAXWELL

Scripture quotations are taken from the HOLY BIBLE: NEW INTERNATIONAL VERSION®. Copyright © 1973, 1978, 1984 by International Bible Society. Used by permission of Zondervan Publishing House.

Cover and text design by Bill Thielker

Printed in the United States of America

ISBN 0-9715828-0-7

CONTENTS

INTRODUCTION
BY DR. JOHN C. MAXWELL

The dictionary uses the word *greatness* to describe something that is "remarkable in degree of effectiveness; distinguished; superior in quality; remarkably skilled." Sound like the kind of life you'd like to have? You can!

Regardless of your GPA, your college destination or your ultimate career path, true greatness is within your grasp. The key to achieving it is not your personality, your temperament, your natural talents or even your present circumstances. The key is your character. If your attitudes and behaviors are "remarkable in degree or effectiveness; distinguished; superior in quality; remarkably skilled;" you can break through barriers, overcome obstacles, transcend limitations and maximize the opportunities that come your way.

The message of this book is vital if you aspire to that kind of greatness. These dynamic pages reveal a blueprint for true success, a plan that is both practical and relevant. I especially appreciate the way each chapter builds upon the others, literally spelling out the essence of true greatness. The rich combination of biblical examples, personal applications and inspirational quotations creates a powerful package. You will discover principles for a lifetime of achievement, plus the strategies to put those principles into practice. Each section concludes with seven steps to achieving greatness in that specific character quality.

Graduate to Greatness is built upon a strong foundation of nine essential concepts expressed in nine key words. Permit me to introduce and comment on those words, which combined spell GREATNESS:

Gratitude. Every truly great person is a grateful person. Any success you experience will be undeniably linked to the people who have been influential and integral to your life. It's vital that you know how and when to express gratitude to them and for them.

Reliability. As a child, I learned a simple saying that has stuck with me: *The best ability is reliability.* This is a true statement; I know so because the Bible says so. The New Testament teaches that the number one priority of Christian stewards is faithfulness, a synonym for reliability. Prove yourself reliable and the doors of opportunity will open wide for you.

Enthusiasm. This quality is so important, yet it is easily misunderstood. Enthusiasm is not excitability. It is much deeper. Even if you have a reserved, quiet personality, you can be enthusiastic because enthusiasm has more to do with inward attitude than outward expression.

Accountability. Right in the middle of the word accountability is a small but significant word: *count.* This word reminds me of three essentials for a disciplined life: First, I must be a person others can *count on.* Second, I must be a person who *counts for* what is right. Third, I must be a person who *counts* *the cost* before taking on a job. Etch these resolutions on your heart and you will learn the power of accountability.

Tenacity. This word makes me think of a strong, relentless grip; and that's exactly what it takes to achieve greatness. Think of all the expressions that reinforce this fact: *Hold on* to your principles. *Hold fast* in all circumstances. *Hold forth* against all obstacles. And, I would add, when you get to the chapter on Tenacity, *hang on* to every word.

Nobleness. Everyone has ambitions in life — to do something, to go somewhere, to be someone. But those basic desires must be driven by the best and purest motives; otherwise life loses its true meaning. Noble ambitions are crucial to experiencing fulfillment and significance.

Excellence. If I had to choose just one word to describe the nature of true greatness, this would be the word. Excellence relates to how you act, how you speak and how you think as you pursue all that life has to offer. And excellence is also the goal; it's the object of your pursuit. "Graduating to Greatness" simply means "escalating to excellence."

Spirituality. You are a spiritual being. Yes, you are made up of flesh and blood and billions of cells; but the true you is spiritual, not physical. This fact demands that you give constant attention to becoming spiritually fit. This is an ongoing, intensive process; but the result is the greatest discovery you can make: finding the will of God.

Servanthood. True servanthood is the heart of true greatness. The perfect model for this virtue was Jesus Christ, who "came not to be served, but to serve, and to give his life as a ransom for many." Being Christ-like in our actions and attitudes demands a passionate concern for other people and a willingness to put them ahead of our own interests. When we do so, something amazing happens. As Jesus explained, the one who is humble will be exalted, and the one who is last will be first. This is a remarkable paradox of the Christian life: the way to greatness is the way of humility.

Why should you aspire to greatness? Certainly not for the purpose of putting yourself on a pedestal or drawing attention to your excellence and superiority. Just the opposite, in fact. True greatness of character does three things: It pleases God, it serves other people, and it satisfies you. How can you lose?

You have exciting days ahead, and I wish you well on your journey. You'll discover that this book is the perfect road map.

John C. Maxwell
Founder, The INJOY Group
Atlanta, Georgia

CHAPTER ONE

ACHIEVING GREATNESS THROUGH

GRATITUDE

FOR ALL BLESSINGS

Imagine that you have an incurable disease, a frightful condition that is slowing eating away your hands, your feet, even your nose. Your skin is painfully dry and encrusted. You've been told there is no hope, no help, nothing you can do. The disease is contagious, so everyone avoids you, fearful that you will infect them, too. Your only companions are nine other people who suffer the same fate. They offer no encouragement because, like you, they have no answers. One day while all of you are huddled together, a great man walks by. They call him the Healer. You've heard the rumors about his great powers. Is it possible that he could set you free from the prison of this sickness?

Your mind reels in all directions. It's been years since you were able to be with your family, to give someone a hug, to shake hands with a friend. Could this man be the answer? It's worth finding out! You shout at him from a distance, "Master, have pity on us!" He looks over and says simply, "Go, show yourselves to the priests." You know what that means, because the priests are the only

Don't kneel to me, that is not right.
You must kneel to God only
and thank Him for the liberty
you will hereafter enjoy.

—Abraham Lincoln's words to a newly freed slave,
following the Emancipation Proclamation

ones who can certify that a person has been healed! Suddenly you're overwhelmed with the possibility of being normal, and all ten of you leave immediately to find the priests. On the way, it happens: your skin clears, your circulation returns, everything is like it's supposed to be! You are healed!

Now what do you do? Rush to your family and announce the amazing news? Shout with joy to everyone you see? Of course. But, first things first. There's someone to see before anyone else, someone to whom you owe the greatest debt of gratitude. You turn around and run joyously to the Healer, falling at his feet and saying "Thank You" with more emotion than you've ever felt before. He looks down and asks, "Where are the other nine?" Then it sinks in: you're all by yourself. Nobody else came with you to say thanks for an inexpressibly wonderful gift. You have no explanation to offer, because such ingratitude is beyond explanation.

This is not an imaginary scenario; it actually happened to Jesus, God's own Son. Luke's Gospel records the story: Ten men, living with the death sentence of leprosy, are suddenly cured. But only one comes back to say "Thank You" to Jesus. Only one out of ten expresses genuine gratitude.[1]

Many people are like the nine lepers who never came back. They fail to live with an attitude of gratitude. They miss the connection between life's blessings and the priority of thankfulness.

What does it mean to have an attitude of gratitude? It's a mindset that is positive, determined and

God gave you a gift of
86,400 seconds today.
Have you used one
to say 'thank you'?

— William Ward

focused. It's a way of approaching every day, relating to every person and dealing with every situation.

Perhaps you remember the old song that says, "Don't worry...be happy." That's a nice thought, but you won't find it in the Bible. However, you will find this one: "Don't worry...be grateful." More specifically: "Don't worry about anything, but be thankful for everything."[2]

Now, maybe you're wondering how it's possible to not worry about anything. The answer is that it's not possible in your ability alone, but it is possible through the power of Christ in you. In other words, He can give you the strength to not worry. And, better yet, He can empower you to be grateful in every circumstance of life.

Every day is an opportunity. In fact, every moment is an opportunity to pursue the greatness of gratitude. William Ward wrote, "God gave you a gift of 86,400 seconds today. Have you used one to say 'thank you'?" His question hits every one of us right in the heart, reminding us that gratitude is an intentional act on our part. It's something we must choose to do, consciously and specifically.

You've travelled life's road for the better part of two decades, and you have untold miles yet to go. How did you get to where you are today? As psychologist Gary Smalley observes, "If you stop to think about it, there are very few benefits in your life for which you can take sole credit." In fact, there may not be any benefits in life for which any one of us can take all the credit!

If we meet someone
who owes us a debt of gratitude,
we remember the fact at once.
How often we can meet someone
to whom we owe a debt of gratitude
without thinking about it at all!

— Goethe

What do you have to be grateful for? If you were to write a lifetime "thank you" list, what would it include? Let me suggest that the first two words you should write are, "Thank God..." Without Him, there is no life — physically or spiritually. Without His grace, there's no reason for living. God is good, He loves you and He's given you two indescribable gifts — His Living Word, Jesus, and His written Word, the Bible. Beyond this, He blesses you with other gifts, each one a compelling reason to say, "Thank God!"

Thank God for the People He has Placed in Your Life. From day one, your life has been filled with people. They have given you their time, their instruction, their interest, their love. Your family has enfolded you with care and concern, day after day meeting your needs. Your teachers have given you knowledge and guided you into new worlds of understanding. Your coaches and mentors have invested themselves in you, believing their efforts will some day pay great dividends as you succeed. Your spiritual leaders have given you godly direction, praying diligently for you and desiring your growth in Christ. Thank God for the people who have shaped your life and those who will continue to influence you.

Thank God for His Provision. Up to this point in life, God has used others to provide for you. The food you eat, the clothes you wear, the house you call home and the bed you call your own were probably paid for by someone else. Should you simply take this for granted as if it's what you have coming to you? After all, isn't it the job of parents to provide? And don't governments exist to give us roads to drive and schools to attend? Perhaps most young men and women do take these things for granted. But what about you? Will you break free from the status quo and practice the attitude of gratitude? When the time comes (and it *will* come) to provide for others, what will you expect from those you provide for? Choose to be grateful and you will enrich your heart and expand your appreciation of life's benefits.

Thank God for His Protection. Ours is a dangerous world, filled with threats and challenges on a global scale and in daily life. The risk of sickness and stress is always just around the corner. The possibility of death is as close as that vehicle speeding in your direction. The potential for problems comes up as sure as the sun. But there is a truth that transcends every threat: the truth that God cares for His own. He even assigns angels to guard you, invisible agents in His service.[3] Most of the time, we have no idea what God has protected us from. That's why it's all the more important to live the attitude of gratitude. Life's problems are real, but so is His protection.

Thank God for His Power. It takes power to make something work. Fuel for an engine, food for the body, electricity to turn the great motors of industry. It takes power to make life work, too — spiritual power. It's the force Paul described when he said, "I can do everything through him who gives me strength."[4] It is the power to face life with full confidence, knowing that the source of your strength is beyond yourself. You are the conduit for a divine current. For that, above all, you should be thankful.

7 STEPS TO GRATITUDE FOR ALL BLESSINGS

Gratitude, like all the great disciplines of life, is a choice. Here are some practical, proven ways in which you can live a grateful life...

 Keep a gratitude journal. The purpose of a gratitude journal is to keep a record of life's blessings and benefits. Write down the names of people who befriend you, encourage you, help you, motivate you, teach you and enrich your life. List the specific ways in which those people have blessed and benefitted you.

 Express your gratitude in definitive ways. Write thank you notes, letters and e-mails. Send flowers. Say thank you verbally and add an "exclamation point" by mentioning a specific way that person is special to you. Give a gift, even a very small one. Do favors frequently without being asked.

 Make thanksgiving a part of your daily prayer. Whenever you pray, think hard about what God is doing in your life and for your life. Be specific and be thankful for His daily provision, protection and power.

 Always give credit where credit is due. Brag on other people, not about yourself. Commend people for a job well done, a meal well prepared, a service well delivered. Never take credit unjustly.

 Say grace at meals. Don't do this as a ritual but as a recognition that every good gift comes from God and that He really is the source of your "daily bread." Jesus took the time to pray over meals, so there's no better example for this important habit.

 Send Thanksgiving cards or make Thanksgiving calls. Contact the people who have had the greatest influence on your life each year. Thanksgiving is an extraordinary opportunity to express gratitude to people who touch your life.

 Do a daily check on your attitude of gratitude. An attitude is more than just a feeling; it's a way of living and thinking. Keep yourself honest and stay with the plan. Don't let a day pass without saying "thank you" to God and to at least one other person.

References:
1 Luke 17:11-19
2 Philippians 4:6
3 Hebrews 1:14
4 Philippians 4:13

CHAPTER TWO

ACHIEVING GREATNESS THROUGH
RELIABILITY
IN ALL CIRCUMSTANCES

The young man stood alone. Behind him, on the side of a mountain, was an army of terrified soldiers. Day after day they had heard the enemy's taunts rumbling across the valley like thunder before a deadly storm. Now the troops watched him, and they had to wonder what was happening. We can only imagine their thoughts...

He's just a kid!
What's he doing out there?
He doesn't have any armor or weapons.
We're in big trouble.

On the opposite mountainside an even larger army was gathered. They were cocky and extremely sure of themselves. They had total confidence in their big man. Indeed he *was* a big man — 9 feet, 6 inches tall. He was their go-to guy, the one who would lead them to victory. Had there been an NBA in those days, he would have been the greatest of superstars. His hands held not a basketball but a sword, a spear and a javelin. The point of the spear alone weighed more than a bowling ball!

If you learn to trust in the Lord,
you will become trustworthy.
If you learn to rely on Him,
you will become reliable.
If you learn to lean on God,
you will become someone
others can lean on.

This big man, Goliath, had issued a challenge: "Send out your best man to fight me. If I win, you will be our slaves. If he wins, we will be your slaves." He had repeated the challenge morning and evening for 40 days. But there had been no takers, and the level of fear and stress among the soldiers had risen increasingly higher. Then the young man showed up unexpectedly. In no time, he sized up the situation and saw the solution: *He* would face the big man.

He had confidence, but he wasn't cocky. He had determination, but he wasn't deceived. The young man, a mere teenager, was ready to engage the battle of a lifetime. His entire nation was relying on him. If he failed, they would lose everything. But if he won, they would overcome an entire enemy force.

The young man, whose name was David, was a simple shepherd boy. He lived in the remote region of Bethlehem, taking care of his father's flock. While tending the sheep, David had already faced giants on two occasions: a giant lion and a giant bear. He killed both animals with his bare hands, knowing very well that God had given him the strength to succeed. Facing the giant Goliath, he knew the power to win would come from that same source.

Victory came very suddenly. As Goliath lumbered down the mountain, David ran toward him, loading his leather sling with a smooth, lethal stone. With practiced precision, he spun the sling in ever-

THE GREATEST POWER
GOD HAS GIVEN US
IS THE POWER
OF CHOICE.

— BILLY GRAHAM

increasing velocity and then released. The stone whistled through the air and smacked rudely into Goliath's forehead. The big man fell flat on his face, and David ran up to finish him off.

David had taken on a huge responsibility — and showed himself to be totally reliable in the toughest of circumstances. He was able to meet an extraordinary challenge because he had extraordinary faith. David had learned firsthand from the author of reliability, God Himself; and in the process, David became "a man after God's own heart."[1]

Like David, you are young and energetic and ready to tackle life's challenges. Like him, you will face giant responsibilities. It's a tough world, and you'll run into a lot of "Goliaths" spewing out threats of one kind or another, attempting to defeat you. Others will look to you, depend on you and entrust much to you. They will give you the opportunity to prove yourself, and your reputation will be on the line. In many cases, you'll have only one chance to demonstrate your trustworthiness.

How will you handle the pressure? When given a chance to show whether you can be trusted, what will you do? These are questions you must think about now, *before* the bigger challenges come. You would be wise to do what David did and become a person after God's own heart.

How did David discover the heart of God? Night after night, out under the stars, he meditated on the greatness of God's creation and character. Day after day, as David faithfully handled seemingly

God is the master of every moment

small responsibilities, he was being prepared for the larger ones to come. As he prayed and thought and reflected on God's Word, and as he depended on God for strength and wisdom in his daily activities, he learned some key truths about God...

God can always be trusted. He is eternally faithful, reliable and true.

God always keeps His word. When He says something, you can believe it.

God always fulfills His promises. Every assurance He gives is an assurance kept.

God is always on time. He is the Master of every moment.

God always tells the truth. What He says is so, without question or doubt.

God always stands up for those who are down. He's the faithful friend who lifts the fallen.

God is perfectly consistent. He is always the same — yesterday, today and forever.[2]

David wanted these godly characteristics in his own life. That was his deepest desire, and that's what made him a person after God's own heart. David wasn't perfect, of course; and he sometimes failed miserably. But he never stopped pursuing the heart of God. He taught his son, Solomon, these same truths; and Solomon expressed many of them in the Book of Proverbs. In Proverbs 3:5-6, Solomon wrote, "Trust in the Lord with all your heart and lean not on your own understanding; in all your ways acknowledge him, and he will make your paths straight." You could read all the books in the world and never find a better statement of purpose or a better creed to live by.

If you learn to trust in the Lord, you will become trustworthy. If you learn to rely on Him, you will become reliable. If you learn to lean on God, you will become someone others can lean on. Ultimately, all confidence is placed in God; but His plan is to live His character through you, and that's why reliability is so important. People need to trust you; they need to count on you to be reliable. In your future education, in your career and in all the relationships life will bring, reliability can make or break your reputation and your effectiveness.

7 STEPS TO RELIABILITY IN ALL CIRCUMSTANCES

Becoming a person whom others can count on is the result of a process — an ongoing process of proving that you are dependable, consistent, loyal, honest and trustworthy. Success comes one step at a time, and it happens as you take the initiative. Keep in mind these habits of highly reliable people...

 Do the job you're given. Whether the responsibility is a small task or an enormous project, focus on what you have to do and do it without wavering or complaint. Nothing great was ever accomplished by a waverer or a complainer.

Keep your word. When you say you'll do something, do it. When you say you'll be somewhere, be there. When you say you'll help somehow, follow through. Four centuries ago, Cervantes observed that "a man's word is his bond." In other words, giving your word is like giving your commitment in writing. It's still true today.

 Respect confidences. When someone shares something with you in confidence, they put a special kind of trust in you. If you break that trust, you risk breaking the relationship and you put your name in jeopardy. Secrets are to be locked away and carefully guarded, unless keeping that confidence would break one of God's laws or result in harm or injury to someone.

 Be on time. One of the wisest habits you can form is the practice of punctuality. Show up late and you may forgive yourself, but don't depend on others to be so flexible. There's an old saying that's worth remembering: "People count up the faults of those who keep them waiting."

 Tell the truth. Every person is constantly faced with the temptation to tell something other than the truth — to exaggerate, to tell a "little white lie," to overestimate or to stretch the facts. Give in to this temptation and you will pay a price that is too high for the little value received.

Mom was right: Always tell the truth because honesty *is* the best policy — and it's essential to being reliable in all circumstances.

 Do what is right. Billy Graham once said, "The greatest power God has given us is the power of choice." God created within us the ability to choose to do right or to do wrong. We aren't robots programmed to behave in a certain way. Think about the awesome power He has given you. How will you exercise that power? Will you choose to do what is right?

 Stand up for those who are down. There is no lasting satisfaction in living for yourself or concentrating on your own interests. Jesus said that even He "did not come to be served, but to serve."[3] He reached out to people in need, to the poor, the disabled, the disenfranchised. He saw people in pain and He was moved with compassion on them.[4] He reached out to those who were down and lifted them up. He set a pattern to follow, a model of reliability that can't be improved upon. Follow that pattern. Live by that model. It will have a remarkable effect on the person you become.

References:
1 Acts 13:22
2 Hebrews 13:8
3 Mark 10:45
4 Matthew 9:36

Chapter Three

Achieving Greatness Through

ENTHUSIASM

In All Opportunities

Enthusiasm is from an ancient word that means "God at work in you." It is a deeply spiritual quality, and we find it throughout the Bible. The writer of Ecclesiastes put it this way: "Whatever your hand finds to do, do it with all your might."[1] The apostle Paul said it like this: "Whatever you do, work at it with all your heart, as working for the Lord, not for men."[2] To be enthusiastic is not to be self-motivated but to be Spirit-motivated. Enthusiasm is a flame which burns bright in you, a driving desire to think higher and better, to believe the positive, not the negative, to choose what is pure over what is popular.

Your life will be filled with opportunities as diverse and colorful as the images in a kaleidoscope. As you seize those opportunities, enthusiasm is vital for so many reasons...

Enthusiasm is contagious. If you are enthusiastic, your attitude will have a contagious effect on others. They will "catch" your upbeat spirit, and they will be influenced by your positive mindset. You may not see the impact, but you can be sure that it happens.

What counts
is not necessarily the size
of the dog in the fight,
but the size of the fight
in the dog.

— Gen. Dwight D. Eisenhower

Enthusiasm gives courage. When you face a problem or deal with a challenging situation, enthusiasm can make all the difference. When you are filled with enthusiasm, it forces out all the negative emotion that can be so demoralizing and defeating. Gen. Dwight D. Eisenhower, who was the Supreme Commander of Allied forces in World War II and later served as President of the United States, knew the encouraging power of enthusiasm. He once said, "What counts is not necessarily the size of the dog in the fight, but the size of the fight in the dog."

Enthusiasm increases determination. If you could put enthusiasm under a microscope, you would see many component parts. One of the most prominent is determination. The enthusiastic person is a determined person — one who has a "can't-quit" attitude. It's a perspective that legendary coach Vince Lombardi described like this: "Winning isn't everything, but *wanting* to win is."

Enthusiasm leads to success. The person *Time* magazine named the greatest man of the 20th century, Sir Winston S. Churchill, was chosen to lead his nation in its darkest hour. When he took command as Britain's Prime Minister in World War II, England was under attack by Hitler's relentless bombers. Churchill knew there would be many dark days and tough losses before final victory was won. But he never lost the enthusiastic belief that his troops would prevail over the Nazi forces. "Success," he wrote at the time, "is going from failure to failure without loss of enthusiasm."

It is the greatest shot of adrenaline
to be doing what you've wanted
to do so badly.
You almost feel like you
could fly without the plane.
— Charles Lindbergh

Enthusiasm has powerful effects.
Enthusiasm, like the biblical grain of mustard seed, will move mountains. It has a powerful effect upon a person's approach to life. If two people have identical abilities and take on an identical task, the one whose attitude is more enthusiastic will inevitably do the better job. As the old saying goes, "knowledge is power, but enthusiasm pulls the switch."

Enthusiasm demands discipline. To keep enthusiasm at a high level it must be nourished with new actions, new aspirations, new efforts and new vision. It demands the discipline of ever-expanding goals and a determination to break your own record or exceed your own expectations.

Enthusiasm gives motivation. Today we take for granted the ability to fly across the world's oceans, but until 1927 that feat was thought impossible. Then a young man named Charles Lindbergh accepted the challenge and set out to prove the skeptics wrong. In a silvery single-engine airplane called "The Spirit of St. Louis," Lindbergh took off from a field in New York, bound for Europe. If he succeeded, he would be the first person to make a solo crossing of the fearsome Atlantic Ocean. He was prepared, but most of all he was motivated by a total sense of enthusiasm. Lindbergh told one reporter, "It is the greatest shot of adrenaline to be doing what you've wanted to do so badly. You almost feel like you could fly without the plane." After a sometimes harrowing 33-hour flight, Charles Lindbergh landed in France and was welcomed by thousands of

Knowledge is power,
but enthusiasm pulls the switch.

well-wishers. History was made — by "The Spirit of St. Louis" and the spirit of enthusiasm.

7 STEPS TO ENTHUSIASM IN ALL OPPORTUNITIES

What about you? How can you "take off" with the spirit of enthusiasm in your life? Here's a flight plan...

 Accentuate the positive. Life will bombard you with all kinds of negative input and influences. It's inevitable and you can't control it. But what you *can* control is your response to what comes your way. You are in charge of your attitude, and it's up to you to be optimistic or pessimistic, to be positive or negative. Accentuate the positive and you will have greater happiness, satisfaction and success than the person who gives in to negative thoughts, emotions and actions.

 Make friends with enthusiastic people. Who you hang out with says a lot about who you are and how you look at life. If you spend a lot of time with non-enthusiastic people, the effects will show. The Bible says that negative friends can corrupt your own thinking and behavior, but positive people will motivate you to do what's best.[3] Again, it's your choice. You can decide who you will spend time with, who you will listen to, who you will share your secrets with. But take care — your companions will influence who you become.

 Divide big projects into several smaller ones. When you begin to work on a big project, enthusiasm can help you get started. It's like a jolt from a powerful battery. But enthusiasm is doubly effective when you couple it with good planning. Being excited about something may get you going down the road, but without a steering wheel you're certain to run into a ditch. Did you ever start a big project that you never finished? Chances are you were excited at the beginning but you failed to reach the goal because you didn't divide the big job into several smaller ones. Don't rely on enthusiasm alone; use the "steering wheel" of good planning to get where you're going in life.

 Just say "no" to gossip. Listening to gossip can be fun, enticing and entertaining. Proverbs 18:8 says that "the words of a gossip are like choice morsels" — tasty bites of food! Unfortunately, those "choice morsels" can give you a really bad case of spiritual indigestion. Gossip will kill your enthusiasm for life and your love for people. By destroying trust and poisoning relationships, it hurts both those who speak it and those who listen to it. The words of the old Spanish saying are true:

"Whoever gossips *to* you will gossip *of* you."

 Be quick to compliment, slow to complain. Do you want people to like you? Do you want to make friends? Then put this principle into practice because it is absolutely effective. Your compliments, of course, must always be genuine and sincere or people will see right through you. As for complaints, follow the advice of Philippians 2:14 and "do everything without complaining or arguing."

 Start and finish every day with an enthusiastic thought. The way you start out will often set your attitude for the whole day. Whether you get up energetically or roll out of bed reluctantly, think first of something positive and uplifting. Meet life with enthusiasm, not reluctance, and you'll reap the benefits. When you go to bed at night, focus your mind on a goal you want to reach or an opportunity you want to strive for. You'll sleep better, and chances are you'll be more focused the next morning.

 Practice the power of enthusiastic thinking. This means more than simply being positive. To think enthusiastically is to think spiritually. Remember, the word *enthusiasm* literally means "God at work in you." Enthusiastic thinking is exactly what

Philippians 4:8 describes: "Whatever is true, whatever is noble, whatever is right, whatever is pure, whatever is lovely, whatever is admirable — if anything is excellent or praiseworthy — think about such things."

References:
1 Ecclesiastes 9:10
2 Colossians 3:23
3 1 Corinthians 15:33

CHAPTER FOUR
ACHIEVING GREATNESS THROUGH
ACCOUNTABILITY
IN ALL RELATIONSHIPS

A very rich man was preparing to leave on a long trip, so he called in three of his employees and gave to each one a large sum of money. To the first one he gave $500,000. To the second he presented $200,000. And to the third he handed over $100,000. The money was not a special bonus or gift; it was a trust — an amount given to each employee to invest as wisely as possible. It was left up to each one to make the most out of what he received. Upon returning from his long trip, the rich man would take account of what each person had done with his money.

The first employee went to work at once, putting the $500,000 into various profit-making ventures. The second employee took his $200,000 and did likewise, choosing smart investments. The third employee, however, took the $100,000 he had been given and drove it into the ground — literally. He went out to the back yard, dug a hole and buried all the money!

Employee #1 was quite successful in his efforts, doubling the $500,000 to a sum of

Every action
of our lives
touches on some chord
that will vibrate
in eternity.
— Edwin Hubbel Chapin

$1,000,000. Employee #2 was equally adept with his investments, turning the $200,000 into $400,000. But Employee #3, who had started out with less in the first place, still had the same $100,000 "safely" buried in the ground.

The rich man returned and eagerly called in the three employees to whom he had entrusted his money. Employee #1 gave his report first, and the rich man was understandably enthused. "I'm giving you a big promotion and a big raise," he said. Employee #2 then presented his account, and once again the rich man reacted gleefully. "You have proven yourself. You're getting a promotion and a raise, too!" Then Employee #3 came in to deliver his report. "Sir," he began, "I know what a tough businessman you are, so I was afraid to risk any of your money. I buried it for safekeeping, and now I'm pleased to return it to you." The rich man was furious. "You lazy bum! The least you could have done was put it in the bank and earn me some interest. So you think I'm a tough businessman? You're right... and you're fired!" Employee #3 was then thrown out of the building, and the rich man took the $100,000 that had been buried and gave it as a bonus to Employee #1.

What you've just read is a modern-day version of a story Jesus told 20 centuries ago.[1] The main point, which hasn't changed in 2,000 years, is that each one of us is personally responsible to make the most of what we've been given. And we are more than responsible; we're *accountable*. In other words, we have to answer for the way we invest our lives.

THE GREATEST THOUGHT
I HAVE EVER HAD
AND THE MOST
IMPORTANT THING
I HAVE EVER LEARNED
IS THAT I AM
PERSONALLY ACCOUNTABL
TO THE GOD
OF ALL CREATION.

— DANIEL WEBSTER
AMERICAN STATESMAN

To whom are you accountable?

You are accountable, first of all, to God.
You are under His authority and you will answer to Him for everything. God is the ultimate judge who will hold you to account for all you do and even for everything you say. Jesus said, "I tell you that men will have to give account on the day of judgment for every careless word they have spoken."[2] God will determine whether you have been a good manager of everything He has put in your care. The Apostle Paul explained: "It is required that those who have been given a trust must prove faithful."[3]

Daniel Webster, the American statesman who was considered by many to be the brightest man of his generation, was once asked, "What is the greatest thought you have ever contemplated?" He replied, "The greatest thought I have ever had and the most important thing I have ever learned is that I am personally accountable to the God of all Creation." Imagine that! You and I (and every other person) will one day face the One who spoke the universe into existence, the One to whom we owe life itself. What an awesome thought, and what a motivation to live the right life, think the right thoughts, speak the right words and do the right things.

You are also accountable to other people. As John Andrew Holmes cleverly wrote, "The entire population of the universe, with one little exception, is composed of others." That "one little exception" is *you*, of course. The fact is, you don't exist in a self-sufficient, isolated world. You belong to a global family; and your success depends upon how you relate to others in that family.

There are some relationships in which the importance of accountability is obvious. To your parents, for example. Your primary duty to them can be summed up in two words: *obedience* and *respect*. That is what God commands and expects, and it is what He will hold you accountable to do. The time will soon come when you are totally on your own and free from parental oversight. When that day arrives, you will no longer have to obey your parents — but you will still owe them your respect. "Honor your father and mother"[4] is a command without a time limit.

Another vital relationship is the one you have with the spiritual leaders in your life — the people God places in Christian authority over you. How should you relate to them? The answer is absolutely clear: "Obey your leaders and submit to their authority. They keep watch over you as men who must give an account. Obey them so that their work will be a joy, not a burden, for that would be of no advantage to you."[5] Notice that just as you are accountable *to them*, they are accountable *for you*.

How does accountability work in all the other relationships of life? What about all your friends, classmates, co-workers, neighbors and acquaintances? Do you really owe these people anything? According to the Bible you do: "Let no debt remain outstanding, except the continuing debt to love one another, for he who loves his fellowman has fulfilled the law."[6]

Yes, you are in debt to others; and the way to pay the bill is by showing them genuine Christian love.

For what are you accountable?

You are accountable for your words. What you say is important to God. It's also important to others, and they will hold you to your words. A promise is meant to be kept, because if you break a promise, you can break a heart. A commitment is meant to be fulfilled, because if you fail on a commitment, you can fracture a friendship. Guard your words; they have great value and great power.

You are accountable for your actions. Every day, you choose to be kind or unkind, to be caring or insensitive, to be positive or negative. You can live by the Golden Rule or by your own rule. The choice is yours. While you are free to choose your actions, you are not free to choose the consequences. You *will* have to answer for what you do.

You are accountable for your opportunities. Every day also brings new opportunities to influence others in word and deed. Christian scholar William Barclay wrote: "In the time we have it is surely our duty to do all the good we can to all the people we can in all the ways we can." This is especially true of your relationship to people who are less fortunate. Albert Schweitzer, a German physician who became a medical missionary to Africa said, "Even if it's a little thing, do something for those who have need of help, something for which you get no pay but the privilege of doing it."

7 STEPS TO ACCOUNTABILITY IN ALL RELATIONSHIPS

Accountability is a key element of a successful life. It is your "track record," the pattern of discipline and dependability that will become your reputation. To be accountable is to be someone others can count on. Here are some practical steps you can take toward building a positively accountable life...

 Keep track of your promises...and keep them. It's so typically human to take other people's promises more seriously than we take our own. Don't make this mistake. If anything, be harder on yourself than you are on others. If you make a promise, be it small or large, keep it. If there is any chance you'll forget it, write it down... and keep your word.

 Maintain a record of your activities, appointments and commitments. No one is capable of remembering every detail of life — all the things to do, places to go, people to meet, etc. It's essential to keep a record so that you can manage life effectively. Use a daily planner or a computer program or create your own system. By all means, don't rely on your mental "computer" alone.

 Be willing to be vulnerable. Accountability in human relationships demands a willingness to be honest, and being honest makes you vulnerable. It can be risky, but it's worth it because the strongest relationships are formed through honest communication. Every one of us has weaknesses and negative tendencies, but through accountability we grow in personal strength and replace the negative with the positive.

Know the qualities of Galatians 5:22-23. These verses include a list of character qualities called "the fruit of the Spirit." When a Christian lives in obedience to God, He produces these qualities in that person. It is the clearest evidence of a truly spiritual, fully accountable life.

Find wise mentors and learn from them. Self-sufficiency will only get you so far. Even the most gifted persons need instruction and input from others who are more knowledgeable. Tiger Woods may be the greatest golfer ever, but he still seeks out the counsel of wise mentors. He does it to be better at golf; how much more we need mentors to be better at life.

Live by the Two Commandments. The heart of the Old Testament teaching is compressed into the rules of life called the Ten Commandments.[7] The first four of those ten rules pertain to our relationship to God and the last six pertain to our relationship to fellow human beings. Jesus summed up the Ten Commandments into Two Commandments that follow the same pattern: Love the Lord with all your heart, soul and mind; and love your neighbor as yourself.[8] Do these two things and your life will be rich beyond measure.

 Get independent "audits" of your accountability. A business owner turns to a CPA for an objective financial analysis. Likewise, you must have people you can turn to for objective personal analysis — people who will give you an honest, helpful "audit" of your personal growth and maturity.

References:
1   Matthew 25:14-30
2   Matthew 12:36
3   1 Corinthians 4:2
4   Exodus 20:12
5   Hebrews 13:17
6   Romans 13:8
7   Exodus 20:1-17
8   Matthew 22:37

CHAPTER FIVE

ACHIEVING GREATNESS THROUGH
TENACITY
IN ALL CHALLENGES

The news was bad, so bad that he sat down and cried when he heard it. His hometown had been destroyed — burned, smashed to pieces and left in ruins by an enemy force. And there he was, hundreds of miles away, in an age long before planes, trains and automobiles. It would take him weeks to get there and require a monumental rebuilding effort once he arrived...but first he had to get permission to go. If his boss said "No" that would be the end of it — his boss was the king and his word was final.

The desperate man was a unique individual named Nehemiah. What would he do in the face of this challenge? How would he convince a world ruler to give him several months off to make a dangerous journey to a distant land? And what was the chance that the king would allow such a thing? You see, Nehemiah was no ordinary servant; he was, in fact, the most trusted man in the palace, the emperor's number one assistant. In the royal court, no one was closer to the king than Nehemiah. His word carried weight, and he was a direct decision-maker for the most powerful

Diamonds
are only
lumps of coal
that stuck to their jobs.
— B. C. Forbes

ruler on earth. It was a role that allowed no room for error, no space for any slip-ups.

Before he talked to the king, Nehemiah first talked to God. With a heavy heart he begged the Lord to help. Days later, Nehemiah boldly asked the king for permission to go. He proposed a schedule and even asked for help in acquiring building materials. The king granted all of Nehemiah's requests. Soon he was off on the trek of a lifetime, bound for Jerusalem.

When he finally arrived, Nehemiah was not greeted by a welcoming party; in fact, what he discovered was a lot of demoralized people in the midst of a destroyed city. The city wall, its most important defensive structure, was in shambles. To make matters worse, enemy forces were occupying the town. At night, when no one was looking, Nehemiah went on a scouting expedition, getting a thorough look at the situation they faced. His mission was clear: *he would lead the effort to rebuild the great wall.*

Nehemiah went to his people and announced that the wall was going to be rebuilt. They rallied around him and the work began. And so did the opposition. Over a two-month period, the attacks came in many forms. First, there was mockery. The opponents pelted them with vicious words. Then came ridicule as the enemies made fun of what Nehemiah and his co-workers were trying to do. Like verbal bullets, the questions came flying, puncturing the validity of their cause. When that tactic failed to work, intimidation came next, followed by

Be like a postage stamp —
stick to one thing
until you get there.
— Josh Billings

extortion, slander, lies, false accusations and rumors. When the wall was half-way done, the attacks were more fierce than ever, including even attempted murder. But Nehemiah was tenacious. He would not give up or give in. Against the tide and against the odds he pressed on until finally, on the 52nd day, the wall was completed. His people were energized, their enemies were defeated and ultimate success was secured.[1]

Nehemiah is a powerful example of leadership, organization and ingenuity; but his most enduring trait is tenacity. He kept going at all costs in all situations; and he inspires us centuries later to practice the power of perseverance. Life has a way of marshalling forces against us, and we must constantly choose to go against the tide or be swept along with it. You have undoubtedly experienced this already. Chances are you've had to deal with obstacles and opposition and difficulty. Perhaps it was an adult who said you didn't have the right qualifications, or a friend who let you down, or a rumor about you that was totally untrue. Maybe it was the challenge of finishing two major projects that were due on the same day. Whatever your challenges have been, they're certain to get even more intense. More than ever, you'll need tenacity.

Whenever you've "got milk" you can thank a man named Louis Pasteur. In the late 1800s, he perfected a process that now bears his name: *pasteurization*. Through pasteurization, milk and other liquids are purified of harmful organisms. It took Pasteur thousands and thousands of failed experiments before

By perseverance
the snail
reached the Ark.

— Charles H. Spurgeon

he finally succeeded. But the great scientist refused to give up, and his determination finally paid off. He wrote to a friend, "Let me tell you the secret that has led me to my goal: my strength lies solely in my tenacity."

You, too, can grow strong through tenacity. To give up is easy, but it is never satisfying. Only if you stick with it will you ultimately prevail. Think about these fascinating examples: The Coca-Cola company sold only 400 Cokes in its first year of business. The first Dr. Seuss book was rejected by 23 publishers before one agreed to print it. Henry Ford went bankrupt twice before hitting it big in the automotive industry. The chemist who perfected Coca-Cola, the author who created Dr. Seuss and the man who invented the modern automobile industry all had one thing in common: they would not give up. With a persistent attitude, they kept trying until they reached their goals. Their example echoes Josh Billings' advice: "Be like a postage stamp — stick to one thing until you get there."

It is a basic rule of life that perseverance pays. Keep pressing forward, even when the going is rough, and eventually you'll arrive. As Charles H. Spurgeon wrote, "By perseverance the snail reached the Ark." In fact, *two* persistent snails made it!

Whenever you're tempted to think of all the reasons you can't hang on, remember that other people have faced even greater problems and still prevailed. Perhaps you know the story of Helen Keller, whose remarkable life was the subject of the famous play, *The Miracle Worker.* Helen Keller was both blind and deaf, yet she lived a full and energetic life. She wrote books, lectured on college campuses, and travelled around the world as a goodwill ambassador. In her memoirs she said, "We can do anything we want to do if we stick to it long enough."

Tenacity is essential to success. You may have talent, but without tenacity it will be wasted. You may even be a genius, but without tenacity it will go unrewarded. True achievement comes through diligent, tenacious, hard work. If you grasp this fact and put it into practice, you will reap the dividends.

7 STEPS TO TENACITY IN ALL CHALLENGES

What does it take to have tenacity? What are the steps to a powerfully persistent life? Here are some of the most important...

Go to the limits of your endurance. Tenacity will energize you to press on even when it seems you have no reserves left. When you're striving to reach a goal, pushing yourself to the limits of your endurance is sometimes the only way to succeed. But once you get there, there's a feeling of tremendous satisfaction. And it will often reveal that your limits are much farther out there than you imagined.

Refuse to be put down by negative thinkers and naysayers. If you have a great idea, a bold project or an innovative concept, it seems there is always someone willing to say it can't be done or shouldn't be attempted. Just say "No" to the naysayers.

 Defeat defeatism. Defeatism is a cancerous attitude that causes people to think they are whipped even before they have begun to fight. Be aware of this mindset and refuse to tolerate it in yourself or be influenced by it in anyone else.

 Don't be surprised or thrown off balance by challenges. Life is full of surprises. Situations change, expectations increase, difficulties arise. It can happen suddenly and unexpectedly. Don't let the unexpected challenge discourage or dismay you. Adapt, redirect your energies if necessary, but don't stop.

 Work harder. Many a problem can be solved and many a challenge can be met simply by working a little harder. Being prepared and willing to meet life head-on means being ready to work as hard as you possibly can.

 Read the biographies of great men and women. Perhaps without exception, great individuals have exercised tenacity in the face of formidable challenges. As you read their stories you will be inspired to persevere as they did.

Stay focused on your purpose. If you know your purpose and you keep it consistently in focus, you will succeed. This begins with knowing your life purpose, and it extends to everything you do. Let your purpose determine your priorities, and let your priorities determine your plans. Follow this pattern and you will realize the great potential for which you were created.

Reference:
1 Nehemiah 1:1-7:3

CHAPTER SIX

ACHIEVING GREATNESS THROUGH

NOBLENESS

IN ALL AMBITIONS

She was so lovely that everyone who saw her was impressed with her great beauty. But most of all they were captivated by her beautiful spirit. There was something extraordinary about her, a depth of character that transcended physical attractiveness. She was young, just a teenager; but she carried herself with regal ease. Everything about her was exceptional, including the traumas she had experienced. Her name was Esther.

Esther was an orphan. As a young child she had lost both of her parents, but a caring uncle named Mordecai raised her as his own child. Above all, Mordecai instilled in Esther the understanding that God loved her and as her heavenly Father would care for her perfectly. She accepted that truth and it empowered her. It gave her confidence and it filled her heart with courage.

One day a very unexpected thing happened to Esther. She was minding her own business, fulfilling her responsibilities, when government representatives showed up at her door. They ordered her to come with them because she had been chosen to be one of the candidates in a

I had ambition
not only to go farther
than any man had ever been before,
but as far as it was possible
for a man to go.

— Captain James Cook

unique beauty contest. The king wanted a new queen, so his top officials had launched a nationwide search to find "Ms. Right."

From the moment she arrived at the palace citadel, Esther won the hearts of those in charge. She was given the best food, the finest perfumes, the most lavish clothing. They just knew she would be the one who would capture the king's heart, too. And they were right. He took one look and was smitten. At an enormous banquet in her honor, the king presented Queen Esther. It was glorious, but trouble was just around the corner.

The king's highest official, a cruel man named Haman, viciously hated the Jews and convinced the king to sign a death decree against them. That was bad news for Esther because she was Jewish (though the king didn't know that). And it was bad for her uncle because Haman had ordered a gallows to be built specifically for Mordecai's execution. Only one person was closer to the king than Haman — his new Queen. Only Esther was in a position to intercede for her people. But to appear before the king without his permission was against the king's own law. She could be killed. She had to chance it and hope that he would understand. Mordecai had told her, "If you remain silent...you and your father's family will perish. And who knows but that you have come to royal position for such a time as this?" Esther's terse reply says it all: "If I perish, I perish."[1]

Fortunately, the king was understanding; and he offered to grant her any request, up to half his kingdom. Esther simply asked, "Grant me my life

One thing I do:
Forgetting what is behind
and straining toward what is ahead,
I press on toward the goal...
— Philippians 3:13-14

and spare my people, because they have been sold for destruction." The king was amazed and enraged that anyone would do such a thing. He demanded to know the culprit behind this plot. Haman was identified as the scoundrel, and the king ordered that he be hanged on the very gallows Haman had built for Mordecai.[2]

Esther epitomizes the key word of this chapter: *nobleness*. To be noble is to possess the most excellent qualities. It describes a person of highest character, ideals or morals. Esther fit this description perfectly, for she was as virtuous as she was beautiful. When confronted by a threatening situation she chose to act with the most noble ambition — to protect and preserve her people.

Ambition can be either positive or negative. What makes the difference is the motive behind it. If the ambition is driven by self-centered, self-promoting motives, it is negative. But if the impetus behind ambition is to honor God and serve others, it is positive and noble. True fulfillment and lasting significance come only through the pursuit of noble ambitions.

The question you have to ask yourself is not only *what* you want to accomplish in life, but *why* you want to do it. It is possible (in fact, it is common) to have a positive ambition with a negative motivation. Suppose, for example, that you want to be accepted at a certain college simply to show up another person who was turned down by the same school. Your ambition to go to college would be positive, but the motivation behind your choice

"Even when I fail,
I succeed;
I've learned 50,000 ways
not to make a light bulb."
— Thomas Edison

would be negative. As Christians, we recognize a higher purpose in all that we do. We live to glorify God and to serve others in His name. It's a calling that touches everything we do, and it influences the goals we set and the plans we make.

Every person has ambitions to do or to be or to attain something in life. For some, those ambitions are simple — to have a decent job, to get married, to own a house, to make an average income. For others, ambitions are more complex — to earn an advanced degree, to invent something new and useful, to explore new sciences, to start a business. Whatever your ambitions happen to be, whether they are simple or grand, it is vital to test each one and ask, How does this ambition fit into God's plan for my life? How does He want me to use this to honor Him and serve others?

You may be wondering, Can't I just do something because I want to do it? Does it really matter what my motive is? Does God really have anything to do with this anyway? These are normal questions, but they are prompted by a limited view of God. J. B. Phillips, in his brilliant book, *Your God Is Too Small*, describes how the wrong concepts of God can influence our thinking. One concept, he says, is God the Policeman, who constantly leans over the balcony of heaven and yells, "Cut that out!" whenever He sees us doing something pleasureful. Phillips eloquently explains that God isn't like this at all, that He wants us to enjoy life fully. As Jesus Himself said, He came to give us abundant life — full and rich and enjoyable.[3]

In the Psalms, David often refers to ambition, which he calls the desires of the heart. In Psalm 37 he gives a simple formula for realizing those desires: "Delight yourself in the Lord and he will give you the desires of your heart."[4] Delighting in God comes first and is the basis for a happy, fulfilling life. To delight in Him means to desire His will above all else, and if you do that His promise is sure: He will give you "the desires of your heart." This parallels exactly what Jesus told His disciples: Seek God's kingdom and His righteousness first, and everything else will be given to you as well.[5]

Captain James Cook, perhaps the greatest seaman in British history, was a man of far-reaching ambition. As a sailor, he piloted huge clipper ships around the globe. As an explorer, he discovered Australia and New Zealand and was the first to navigate the Great Barrier Reef. As a Christian, Captain Cook was esteemed as a man of integrity and character. In his journals, he once wrote, "I had ambition not only to go farther than any man had ever been before, but as far as it was possible for a man to go." Indeed he did go far and he realized the desires of his heart; but he considered his greatest achievement the work he had done as a scientist. Through his intensive and exhaustive experimentation, Captain Cook discovered the cure for scurvy, the disease dreaded most by men at sea. He could have selfishly exalted in his accomplishments as an explorer, but he focused instead on the satisfaction of helping others and extending their lives. He was a man of noble ambition.

What is your ambition? What is the desire of your heart? As you think about these important questions, consider these steps...

7 STEPS TO NOBLENESS IN ALL AMBITIONS

 Remember that you're in a race. Life is the ultimate marathon, a long distance race over all kinds of terrain in all manner of conditions. As you run this race in pursuit of your ambitions, keep in mind the testimony of the apostle Paul: "One thing I do: Forgetting what is behind and straining toward what is ahead, I press on toward the goal..."[6] Follow his example: he kept running, and he never lost sight of the ultimate goal.

 Deal with today's reality before tackling tomorrow's possibility. It is good to be forward-thinking, just so it is not at the expense of doing first things first. As Winston Churchill counseled, "It is a mistake to look too far ahead. Only one link in the chain of destiny can be handled at a time."

 Read the stories of people who were driven by noble ambitions. When you study those who have achieved great things in serving God and man, their experience will influence your own ambitions.

Don't look at goals as ends in themselves. When you reach a goal, life does not stop. There is satisfaction in achievement; however, a goal is not an end in itself but a transition point to other goals. The finish line for one is the starting line for another.

Be willing to try and be willing to fail. An old adage says that if you aim at nothing you are certain to succeed. It's true. Don't fear attempting new things or trying to master new skills; and don't fear failure. Thomas Edison, history's greatest inventor, said that failure was his friend. He once told a reporter, "Even when I fail, I succeed; I've learned 50,000 ways not to make a light bulb."

Aim high. In archery, as in life, it is essential to aim high. Henry Wadsworth Longfellow wrote, "If you would hit the mark, you must aim a little above it." Don't be afraid to set your sights high.

Delight yourself in the Lord. To experience the greatest personal delight, seek first to please God and do His will. It is the one true way to realize the greatest desires of your heart.

References:
1 Esther 4:16
2 Esther 7:1-10
3 John 10:10
4 Psalm 37:4
5 Matthew 6:33
6 Philippians 3:13-14

CHAPTER SEVEN

ACHIEVING GREATNESS THROUGH
EXCELLENCE
IN ALL ENDEAVORS

Imagine someone your age being appointed as Chief of Staff for the President of the United States. That's the kind of position a young man named Daniel was given, and he did his job with remarkable skill. Everyone was impressed with his wisdom, knowledge and discernment. He made strategic decisions and sound judgments. The Bible says that Daniel had "a spirit of excellence" in him.[1] He was so committed to God and committed to excellence that he was able to achieve astonishing success.

Best of all, Daniel never forgot his faith or failed his God. Of course, there were people who didn't want him to succeed. They were jealous of Daniel and cooked up an evil plot against him. Their plan was wickedly simple: get the king to declare that no one could pray to anyone but the king himself for 30 days. Anyone guilty of breaking this new law would be put to death by being thrown into a pit full of hungry lions.

The king agreed to sign the law, and Daniel's enemies had succeeded in setting the trap. What would Daniel do? Would he change his habit of

If a man write a better book,
preach a better sermon,
or make a better mousetrap than his neighbor,
though he build his house in the woods,
the world will beat a path to his door.
— Ralph Waldo Emerson

openly praying to God? Would the threat of capital punishment keep him from doing what was right? No. In fact, he never hesitated or thought twice about it. His "spirit of excellence" would not allow him to keep his faith a secret. Just as he had always done, Daniel opened his windows toward Jerusalem, got down on his knees and prayed to God.

As expected, Daniel's enemies brought charges against him and presented the undeniable evidence of his "crime." The king, realizing that he had been entrapped by his own decree, wanted to help Daniel. But the law could not be changed, and Daniel was thrown into the den of ravenous lions.

You know how the story ends, of course: God miraculously shuts the lions' mouths and Daniel is spared from certain death. The king orders that he be brought up out of the pit and that all of Daniel's accusers be thrown to the wild animals.[2]

Daniel demonstrated his commitment to excellence in good times and bad. When the new law was pushed through, Daniel knew that sharing his faith publicly would get him into big trouble, but he refused to allow negative people to give him a negative attitude. He had formed a good habit and he wasn't about to break it because circumstances had changed. He was the same person *before, during* and *after* this vicious attack against him. And, in the end, he was the winner.

It's always easier to go with the flow, to follow the crowd, to conform to current trends. You'll discover that most people, in fact, are willing to go

Be a yardstick of quality.
Some people aren't used
to an environment
where excellence is expected.
— Steve Jobs
Founder of Apple Computer

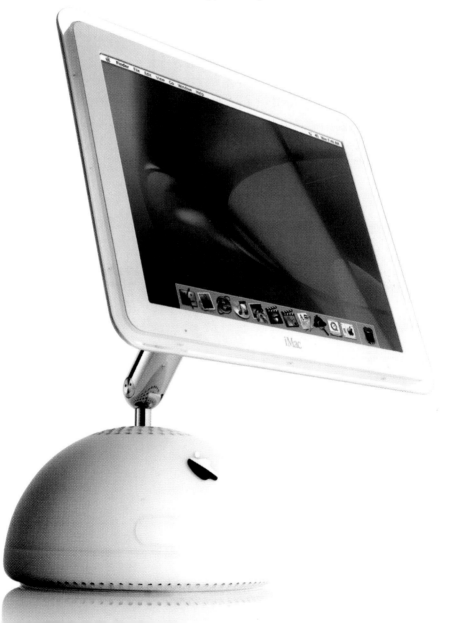

through life that way. They don't want to strive for a higher standard or push themselves beyond the "normal" expectations. They would rather take the easy road, settling for what is acceptable when they could have what is exceptional. The way of excellence is a different path. It is a more difficult road, unpaved and often blocked by obstacles. But it is the better way, and it offers the greatest journey and the most spectacular views.

When you decide to take the path of excellence, you are deciding to strive for the highest and best that you can achieve. You are making a conscious choice to push yourself to the limits in order to realize the full potential of all God has given you. Striving for excellence will place four undeniable demands on you — demands for discipline, determination, discernment and devotion.

The Demand of Discipline. Perhaps no other word is charged with more positive/negative energy than the word *discipline*. Negatively, it can make you think of a parent's correction or a coach's rebuke. But positively, *discipline* can evoke images of a superbly trained athlete or a gifted musician. In your pursuit of excellence, discipline means first of all, forming the right habits. To attain excellence in any endeavor requires consistent, intensive effort. As Aristotle wrote some 2400 years ago, "Quality is not an act. It is a habit." In other words, quality (a synonym for excellence) results not from a one-time attempt but from an ongoing performance. Excellence also requires staying on the right path. One who constantly takes detours down the easy

If people knew
how hard I have had to work
to gain my mastery,
perhaps it would not seem
so full of wonder.

— Michelangelo

road will never reach the summits because they are accessible only on the road of excellence.

The Demand of Determination. When you listen to an accomplished musician, beneath the notes you can probably hear the sound of determination. When you look at a complex blueprint prepared by an architect, you are examining the result of determination. When you admire the work of a gifted designer or painter or sculptor, you are enjoying the product of determination. Regardless of one's chosen pursuit, it is impossible to achieve greatness apart from a relentlessly determined spirit and a never-give-up attitude. Determination doesn't come easily or readily; in fact, it takes work. The great Renaissance artist Michelangelo once wrote, "If people knew how hard I have had to work to gain my mastery, perhaps it would not seem so full of wonder." He wasn't putting himself down; rather, he was underscoring the fact that excellence comes with a price — the price of determined, diligent work.

The Demand of Discernment. To discern is to wisely separate or distinguish, to perceive what is true vs. untrue, pure vs. impure, excellent vs. inferior. *Webster's* dictionary defines discernment as the ability "to detect with senses other than vision." Discernment enables you to choose what builds up over what tears down. It is the quality that selects what is best over what is merely passable. In fulfilling your commitment to excellence, discernment is essential. And, as you do that which is best and follow the higher way, others will take notice. As the great American author Ralph Waldo Emerson observed: "If a man write a better book, preach a better sermon, or make a better mousetrap than his neighbor, though he build his house in the woods, the world will beat a path to his door."

The Demand of Devotion. You've probably heard someone say, "She's really devoted to her studies" or "He's totally devoted to his job." Devotion is one of the hallmarks of excellence. It is the commitment to concentrate on the essentials rather than getting distracted by the nonessentials. Samuel Johnson, the most esteemed English writer of the 18th century, said, "Those who attain excellence commonly spend life in one pursuit; for excellence is not often gained upon easier terms." Johnson's "one pursuit" was to be the finest wordsmith of his generation. He devoted himself to that goal and became a journalist, poet, essayist and lexicographer. Your "one pursuit" in life may be in accounting or business or education or some other field. It really doesn't matter *where* you concentrate your energies, but it matters very much *how* you concentrate them. As fabled football coach Vince Lombardi observed, "The quality of a man's life is in direct proportion to his commitment to excellence, regardless of his chosen field of endeavor."

The path to excellence is challenging, yet so rewarding. Here are some of the steps along the way...

7 STEPS TO EXCELLENCE
IN ALL ENDEAVORS

The purpose in striving for excellence is not to attain perfection but to achieve quality — the highest quality of which you are capable. Excellence is the result of a lifelong pursuit that touches every area of life. As you mature, excellence shines through your words, your actions, your reactions and your attitudes. Others will look at you and see what they saw in Daniel — a "spirit of excellence." Here are some of the essentials...

 Strive for verbal excellence by increasing your word power. People will judge you by the way you use or misuse the English language. Resist being satisfied with what you already know. Expand your vocabulary. Refine your speech. Read a "how-to" book to improve your verbal effectiveness.

 Strive for physical excellence by following a fitness plan. Do whatever it takes to get in shape and stay in shape. Being in top physical condition often facilitates excellence in other areas.

 Strive for social excellence by cultivating your contacts. Along life's path you will meet and greet thousands of people. Many of those contacts can be cultivated into meaningful friendships, but it is up to you to make it happen. Master the art of remembering names, write them down later and keep track of the people you meet.

Strive for intellectual excellence by learning something new every year. Keep your mind fresh and active. Think about the things you would like to experience or the skills you would like to possess. Choose one...set a goal...make a plan... then do it.

Strive for educational excellence by continuing to think of yourself as a student. Even when you're no longer enrolled in some institution, be a student in the school of life. See every day and every opportunity as a chance to learn, to excel, to pursue the best.

Strive for vocational excellence by doing your work with diligence. Remember the advice of Steve Jobs, the founder of Apple Computer: "Be a yardstick of quality. Some people aren't used to an environment where excellence is expected."

Strive for spiritual excellence by growing in the grace and knowledge of Jesus Christ. Make it a priority to spend time every day reading and thinking about the Bible. It is the ultimate guidebook for your journey to complete maturity.

References:
1 Daniel 6:3
2 Daniel 6:4-28

Chapter Eight

Achieving Greatness Through

Spirituality

in All Decisions

Life is a constant stream of decisions. From the moment you awake in the morning until you lie down at night you make one choice after another. What to wear. What to eat. What to do. Where to go. Who to call. When to act. How to react. And the list goes on and on. Some decisions are easy, and you make them readily and spontaneously. Others are quite difficult, especially life's big decisions about college, career, marriage and family. Those are the tough ones you struggle over: Where should I go to college? What kind of career am I cut out for? Who will I marry? *Will* I marry? Where should I live? And beyond these are the gut-level questions about what matters most in life: What is my purpose? What does God want me to do? How can I be sure my life will count?

It is necessary and fitting that this chapter be about decision making, specifically the importance of spirituality in all decisions. *Spirituality* is a word that is used very liberally today, and it means different things to different people. Talk-show hosts, best-selling authors, social leaders, even billionaire business-

GOD HAS PROMISED
TO SUPPLY
ALL YOUR NEEDS,
NOT SOLVE
ALL YOUR PROBLEMS.

men have something to say about spirituality. But what does it mean to you as a Christian? How can you be a person who makes spiritually wise decisions?

Let's take a closer look at that word, *spirituality*. The key to understanding this term is found in the first six letters: *spirit*. That's a vital word in the Bible; in fact, it describes God Himself: "God is spirit, and his worshipers must worship in spirit and in truth."[1] God is a trinity made up of the Father, Son and Holy Spirit. As Christians, we are guided by God's Spirit.[2] He empowers us to serve Him, to do what is right, to be wise in thought and word and deed. Spirituality is simply Spirit-directed living. And spirituality in decision-making happens as you rely on God's Holy Spirit for His guidance. As you do so, His promise is sure: "If any of you lacks wisdom, he should ask God, who gives generously to all without finding fault, and it will be given to him."[3]

If you could only work one passage of Scripture into your future, this would be the perfect choice: "Trust in the Lord with all your heart, and lean not on your own understanding; in all your ways acknowledge Him and He will direct your paths."[4] These power-packed words from Proverbs contain three priorities for effective spiritual living.

Priority #1 is found in the phrase, *Trust in the Lord with all your heart. Trust* is a synonym for *faith*. William Tyndale, the man who first translated the Bible into modern English, defined faith as "acting on the promises of God." This is the essence of trusting the Lord with all your heart — to act not on blind superstition, but on the certainty of God's promises. The Bible defines faith as the substance of things hoped for, the evidence of things not seen.[5] It is believing, counting on and living as if the promises God has made are going to be kept. In short, it is *Acting on the Promises.*

What are some things God has promised you? Here are just a few: He has said He will come and live inside you when you trust Him as your Savior.[6] He has promised to "never leave you or forsake you."[7] He has promised to supply all your needs according to what He has available — His very own riches.[8] And He has promised that if you seek first the Kingdom of God and His righteousness all the essential provisions of life will be added to you.[9] Do you believe that He can do all that? Do you believe He *will* do all that for you? Are you living like it? That's what faith is. That's what it means to "trust in the Lord with all your heart."

Priority #2 is wrapped up in the second phrase, *lean not on your own understanding.* This priority can be summed up as, *Avoiding the Pitfall.* The pitfall is revealed in three words: "your own understanding." Self is the pitfall. When faced with a problem, challenge, need or opportunity, the normal human urge is to figure your own way out, to design your own solution, to depend upon yourself. Self says lean on what you know. Self says lean on what you have. Self says lean on what you are. But God says very clearly, don't lean on yourself. The reason is simple: leaning on self is the opposite of living by faith. God wants you to lean on Him.

To lean on your own understanding is to deny God's authority and direction for your life. The Bible tells us about several people who did that. Abraham leaned on self...he convinced his wife Sarah to lie, and it placed her life in jeopardy and the future of a nation at risk. Jacob leaned on self...he schemed and deceived and it damaged his family relationships and drove him into exile. Moses leaned on self...he took justice into his own hands, and it drove him into a barren place on the backside of the desert for 40 years. David leaned on self...he conned himself into thinking that his pleasure came first, and it drove him to adultery and murder.

To keep from leaning on self, remember this: Depend on what God knows and what He longs to reveal to you. Trust in what God owns and what he longs to provide for you as His child. Rely on what God has done to enable you to live. This is what Paul meant when he said, "I can do everything through him who gives me strength."[10]

So, instead of relying on self, put into practice **Priority #3**, which is discovered in the final phrase, *in all your ways acknowledge Him*, best described as *Acknowledging the Person*. This word *acknowledge* is a term of great intimacy that means to be fully aware, fully appreciative and fully knowledgeable. To acknowledge the Lord in all your ways is to ensure that He (the *Person*, not some impersonal "It" out there in the heavens) is central to everything you think and say and do. It means to recognize His lordship over every aspect of your life. You do this

He is no fool
who gives what he cannot keep
to gain what he cannot lose.
— Jim Elliot

by yielding to His will, praying for His guidance and serving Him with an obedient spirit. When you have a decision to make, it isn't simply *your* decision; since He is your Lord, it's your decision for His sake.

Acknowledging the Person requires that you respect the importance and the intimacy of your relationship with God. As in any significant relationship, communication is key. You cannot know another person without meaningful, constant communication. And to enrich that communication there must be true commitment. To acknowledge the Lord in this way is to be more concerned about what He thinks than you are about what anyone else thinks.

The result of living by these three priorities from Proverbs 3 — Acting on the Promises, Avoiding the Pitfall, Acknowledging the Person — is that *He will direct your paths.* As you go down life's road, He will be your guide. His direction is sure. When you falter and fail and your life gets out of alignment (which is inevitable), He will straighten things out. In your inadequacy, He will be totally adequate, carrying you on to true success and fulfillment.

In 1955, Jim Elliot and his wife, Elisabeth, left the comforts of America and journeyed to Ecuador to serve as pioneer missionaries. Deep in the jungles of that South American country, they set up a base camp with three other couples. Their objective was simple: to make contact with the feared Auca Indians. The Aucas were a tribal people who had never heard the name of Jesus nor interacted with any outsiders. Jim and the three other men in their group made an initial contact which was apparently successful. A few days later, they returned for a second visit, landing their small plane on the river near the Auca encampment. Suddenly, without warning, the Aucas attacked the four young missionaries and slaughtered them. When they failed to return, a search party was sent out to locate the men. They found a scene of vicious brutality.

Understandably, there was outrage at the murder of four promising young men. Many found their actions to be senseless and irresponsible. But even more astonishing was the response of Elisabeth Elliot and the other widows. They decided to continue the mission, to continue to reach out to the Aucas who had killed their loved ones and tell them the Good News of Jesus. Remarkably, the Aucas not only received them, but they received the Gospel as well. A majority of the tribe turned from idolatry to serve the true, living God.

In the journal of Jim Elliot a wealth of insights was discovered after his death. Perhaps most poignant of all is one statement that captures the meaning of sacrifice: "He is no fool who gives what he cannot keep to gain what he cannot lose." Jim Elliot had learned the timeless truth that if you trust in the Lord with all your heart, lean not on your own understanding and acknowledge Him in all your ways, He *will* direct your paths.

7 STEPS TO SPIRITUALITY IN ALL DECISIONS

 Read the Bible daily. Take a few minutes at some point every day to read a brief passage from the Bible. The regular input of God's Word will make a difference in *how* you think and *what* you think. Try this method: read five Psalms and one chapter of Proverbs each day. In 30 days you will complete both books.

 Study the Bible regularly. Do some in-depth examination of the Scriptures. Look for promises to claim, commands to keep and warnings to heed. Never forget that you are studying the Word of God, not just another book. It is God's unique message to you.

 Memorize the Bible faithfully. Store away the Scripture in your mind and heart. It will keep you from sin and false beliefs, it will fill your heart with joy and it will give you spiritual victory.

 Pray when you get up every morning. Jesus had this habit, so it is obviously a good one. At the start of every day, focus your thoughts on God. Commit the day to Him and ask for His blessing and guidance.

Pray whenever you must make big deci-sions. Before He faced the most crucial day of His life, Jesus spent a night in prayer and urged His disciples to do like-wise. When you are faced with a major decision, rely on God's promise of wisdom without limits.

 Pray whenever you are pressured. When you feel the pressure building, when you sense the stress increasing, it is time to pray. Beyond all the demands of life that we can see there rages a spiritual battle that we cannot see. Through prayer we engage God's power to fight that battle and win.

 Remember God's promises and provi-sion. Every major decision you make is an opportunity to remember how God has blessed and guided you in the past. As you live by His promises and in His power you will graduate to the greatness of all He has planned for you.

References:
1 John 4:24
2 John 14:15-26
3 James 1:5
4 Proverbs 3:5-6
5 Hebrews 11:1
6 Colossians 1:27
7 Hebrews 13:5
8 Philippians 4:19
9 Matthew 6:33
10 Philippians 4:13

CHAPTER NINE

ACHIEVING GREATNESS THROUGH

SERVANTHOOD

IN ALL SITUATIONS

If you were to read the list of his accomplishments, you would say without hesitation that he was a "great" man. What he achieved is simply mind-boggling...

He learned, entirely on his own, 34 complex Asian languages.

He, along with a team that he recruited, translated the Bible into all of those languages.

He founded a college which is still an influential institution over 200 years later.

He formed over 100 schools to educate poor girls in a nation where no such schools had existed.

He published the first newspaper in India, a publication which is still the leading paper in a nation of one billion.

He established hundreds of churches in places where the Gospel had never been preached.

The man who did all these things was William Carey. He was extraordinary, but believe it or not, he had a lot of things going against him. Carey grew up in England in the late 1700s, the son of a poor weaver. He had no formal education beyond age 12 when he became a shoemaker's apprentice. He worked in that humble occupation but studied the Bible at every opportunity, usually by candlelight late into the night. Believing that God had called him to the ministry, young William applied for ordination but was rejected. After two more years of trying, he was finally accepted and ordained. As a pastor in a small English village, he continued to study God's Word, and he became convinced that God was leading him to take the Gospel to people who had never heard the Good News. In a sermon he preached at that time, Carey said that Christians should "expect great things from God, and attempt great things for God." It became the motto for the rest of his life.

Leaving behind his country, his family and all that he had ever known, William Carey sailed with his wife and children to India. Arriving in that foreign land he began a work which is now legendary but was then both tough and tragic. He endured persecution from those who resisted the Gospel and opposition from businessmen who didn't want him to convert the heathen. He and his family were stricken with disease. William and his wife survived, but their little son died. He worked for seven years before seeing the first convert to Christianity, but throughout those unimaginably difficult years, Carey kept going — determined to expect great things from God and attempt great things for God.

The greatness that William Carey sought was not recognition for himself or acclaim for his achievements. In fact, he didn't care how highly people thought of him, so long as they thought highly of his Lord. Carey saw himself as a servant, called to honor God, to do His will and to fulfill His purposes. He desired to attempt "great" things because it was for a "great" cause, far beyond what could ever be measured or imagined.

William Carey was profoundly influenced by the words of Jesus to His disciples in Mark's Gospel, chapter 10. Two of Jesus' followers, James and John, had come to Him and asked point-blank, "Can we be the top two guys in your Kingdom, one of us at your right and the other at your left?" Jesus replied, "You don't know what you are asking." And then the other 10 disciples, hearing what was being discussed, exploded with anger at James and John — not because they were humble but because they, too, wanted to be "great" in Jesus' kingdom! Jesus called them all together and said, "Whoever wants to become great among you must be your servant, and whoever wants to be first must be slave of all. For even the Son of Man did not come to be served, but to serve, and to give his life as a ransom for many."[1]

True greatness is found in true servanthood. This is an essential fact of the Christian life. It's the principle that governs every situation in which you must choose between putting yourself first or giving that position to someone else. In a society that is consumed with the idea of "looking out for #1" and making sure that you "get everything that's coming to you" the idea of putting others first is radical. But

Expect great things from God... Attempt great things for God.

— William Carey

that's what Jesus did, and that is how He expects us to live. Whenever you see those now-famous initials W-W-J-D (What Would Jesus Do?) remember that the answer is revealed in the Apostle Paul's letter to the Philippians, where he writes,

"Your attitude should be the same as that of Christ Jesus: Who, being in very nature God, did not consider equality with God something to be grasped, but made himself nothing, taking the very nature of a servant, being made in human likeness. And being found in appearance as a man, he humbled himself and became obedient to death — even death on a cross!"[2]

This is amazing! Jesus made Himself nothing. He became a servant (literally, a slave). He, the God of the universe, humbled Himself to the point of death. And this is the attitude we are supposed to have! How can this be possible? It is possible only because He gives us the strength to be humble and obedient to the Father's will. But we still have to choose, and the great paradox is that when we choose to honor Him and put others first, He chooses to bless our humility and give us a place of honor. This is what God the Father did in response to the humility and obedience of His Son, Jesus:

"Therefore God exalted him to the highest place and gave him the name that is above every name, that at the name of Jesus every knee should bow, in heaven and on earth and under the earth, and every tongue confess that Jesus Christ is Lord, to the glory of God the Father."[3]

7 STEPS TO SERVANTHOOD IN ALL SITUATIONS

 Value approval from the Lord more highly than applause from people. Acclaim from people can be almost intoxicating. Whether their applause is literal or figurative, it can inflate the ego all out of proportion. If you've done a good job or achieved something special, acknowledgement from others is all right, so long as you have worked with the right motive and not just for their praise. What matters most is the Lord's approval because He is the master and you are the servant — His servant.

 Expect great things from God, attempt great things for God. Expectation is a by-product of faith. When you are truly trusting in God, when your faith is in Him alone, it is "normal" to expect greatness of blessing from Him. But, as the Book of James says, "Someone will say, 'You have faith; I have deeds.' Show me your faith without deeds, and I will show you my faith by what I do."[4] This is where the other side of the equation comes in: attempting great things for God — doing everything possible to please Him and to fulfill His purpose in your life.

Seek a high purpose above a high position. Jonathan, the son of King Saul, was a victorious warrior and heir to the throne. But he gave it all up and became a servant to the teenage shepherd boy, David. Jonathan humbled himself even to the point of risking his life so that young David would be elevated into the position God had chosen for him.[5] As a humble servant devoted to Jesus Christ, always seek a high purpose above a high position. Let God do the choosing, and let Him place you in the position He has chosen for you.

 Take inventory of your attitudes. In your relationships with other people, how are you showing concern for their needs and feelings? Are you gentle or harsh? direct or indirect? considerate or forceful? Be honest with yourself as you resolve to show a Christ-honoring, humble sensitivity to the people in your life.

 Forgive and forget. Once you have forgiven someone, imagine that you have taken the offense and thrown it off a high bridge into deep waters, never to be retrieved. In Christ you are fully forgiven. Be fully forgiving of others.

 Practice the paradoxes. A paradox is a statement that is true although it appears to contradict common sense. There were many paradoxes in the teaching of Jesus.

He said, for example: To find your life you must lose it.[6] To be rich you must be poor.[7] To live you must die.[8] And, of course, the two paradoxes that we've discovered in this chapter: To be first you must be last[9], and to be honored you must be humbled.[10] The way to greatness is the way of humility.

 Look out for #1, but remember who #1 really is. When our secular society speaks of "looking out for #1" they're talking about self. By that reasoning, You are #1. But as a Christian you realize that #1 is actually Jesus Christ, not you. And, as Colossians 1:18 reminds us, "in everything He must have the supremacy." Put Him first in your heart because He alone deserves to be first. Serve Him with all your energy because He gave His all for you. Love Him with all your being, for He loved you first.

As you go from this day forward, remember these truths, live by them, and graduate to the greatness of God's abundant blessing on your life.

References:
1 Mark 10:17-28
2 Philippians 2:5-8
3 Philippians 2:9-11
4 James 2:18
5 1 Samuel 18-20
6 Matthew 10:39
7 Matthew 5:3
8 Luke 17:33
9 Matthew 19:30
10 Matthew 23:12